Grizzly 399

and Her Four Hungry Cubs

By Sylvia M. Medina

Photography by Thomas D. Mangelsen

Illustrations by Morgan Spicer

green kids club

NoahText®

Noah Text®

The **Noah Text®** Chapter Books have been carefully selected and curated to meet the needs of all readers – and striving and struggling readers in particular – by providing superior text accessibility. Noah Text® books are rendered in **Noah Text®, a patented evidence-based methodology for displaying text that increases reading skill.**

Grounded in the science of reading, Noah Text® is a specialized scaffolded text that shows **syllable patterns** within words by highlighting them with bold and unbold and marking **long vowels** (vowels that "say their own names"). Here are some examples:

entertainment	⇨	**en**ter**tain**ment
beautiful	⇨	**beau**ti**ful**
photosynthesis	⇨	**ph**o**t**o**syn**the**sis**
comprehension	⇨	**com**pr**e**hen**sion
ironic	⇨	**i**ron**ic**
lieutenant	⇨	**lie**u**ten**ant**
achievement	⇨	a**chie**ve**ment**
epitome	⇨	**e**pit**om**e
ideology	⇨	**i**d**e**o**logy**
coordination	⇨	**c**o**o**rdin**a**tion

By showing readers the structure of words, Noah Text® enhances reading skills, freeing up cognitive resources that readers can devote to comprehension. Noah Text® simulates simpler writing systems (e.g., Finland's) in which learning to read is easier due to visible, predictable word patterns. As a result, Noah Text® increases reading fluency, stamina, accuracy, and confidence while building skills that transfer to plain text reading.

Highly recommended by structured literacy specialists, Noah Text® is effective for developing, struggling, and dyslexic readers and for multilingual learners. Noah Text® enables resistant and struggling readers to advance their reading skills beyond basic proficiency so that they can tackle higher-level learning.

Readers find Noah Text® intuitive and easy to use, requiring little to no instruction to get started. A sound key that further explains how Noah Text® works can be found at the back of this book.

For further information on Noah Text® and its products, please visit www.noahtext.com.

Dear Parents, Educators, and Striving English-Language Readers,

As individuals develop the ability to read beyond the elementary level, their challenge is to build on a basic awareness of how patterns of letters stand for sounds and how those sounds come together to make words. Readers who learn the letter patterns in one-syllable words are poised to recognize them in longer, multisyllable words.

For struggling readers, however, long words can appear to be a sea of individual letters whose syllable sub-divisions are hard to discern. This series from Noah Text® highlights where syllable breaks occur, while also signaling long vowels -- those that "say their own names."   These visual cues help struggling readers decode words more easily and read more fluently and accurately.

Now, with Noah Text® Chapter Books, all individuals can learn to read with less effort, empowering them to experience enriching literature and enlightening informational texts.

Miriam Cherkes-Julkowski, Ph.D.
Professor, Educational Psychology (retired)
Educational Diagnostician and Consultant

About the Author - Sylvia M. Medina is the president, primary author, and creative lead of the Green Kids Club. She has spent her career focused on environmental issues and helping to preserve animal welfare. She hopes to teach children the importance of helping to save our world and its animals.

About the Photographer - Thomas D. Mangelsen is an American nature and wildlife photographer and conservationist. He is most famous for his photography of wildlife in the Greater Yellowstone Ecosystem. He has been active in the movement to keep the Yellowstone area grizzly bears on the Endangered Species List.

About the Illustrator – Morgan Spicer is the founder of Bark Point Studio. She lives a vegan life in NJ, with her 6 rescue dogs and husband. Morgan has illustrated over 40 books and has created thousands of custom portraits since graduating from Syracuse University in 2012.

The following organizations contribute to saving animals and our world:
The Cougar Fund - cougarfund.org
Wyoming Wildlife Advocates - www.wyowild.org
Love the Wild Foundation - www.lovethewild.org

Contributors - Kristin Combs, Tiffany Talbott, Shelley Mascia, and Joy Eagle

green kids club
www.greenkidsclub.com

Grizzly 399

and Her Four Hungry Cubs

By Sylvia M. Medina

Photography by Thomas D. Mangelsen

Illustrations by Morgan Spicer

green kids club

Noah Text®

CONTENTS

Grizzly 399

Summer was **n<u>ea</u>r**ly <u>o</u>ver, and **Griz**zly 399 was t<u>i</u>red and **hun**gry – but **m<u>o</u>s**tly **hun**gry. The sun hung l<u>o</u>w on the **ho**r<u>i</u>**zon**, and the **shad<u>o</u>ws** of the p<u>i</u>nes grew long. The gr<u>ea</u>t be<u>a</u>r thought sh<u>e</u> heard **hunt**ers' guns in the **dis**tance.

Sh<u>e</u> stuck her big be<u>a</u>r snout in the <u>ai</u>r, **h<u>o</u>p**ing to catch a whiff of fresh elk **car**cass. Ah, there it is! sh<u>e</u> thought.

Sh<u>e</u> p<u>ee</u>red thro<u>u</u>gh the brush to s<u>ee</u> if **an**y **hunt**ers were **a**round. There were thr<u>ee</u> men on the **op**po**site** s<u>i</u>de of the **riv**er, who then **dis**ap**p<u>ea</u>red in**to the woods, **drag**ging a dead elk **b<u>e</u>h<u>i</u>nd** them. **Eve**ry fall, sh<u>e</u> saw th<u>e</u>se men with their big, loud guns. Sh<u>e</u> was <u>u</u>sed to **s<u>ee</u>**ing them. As sh<u>e</u> **qu<u>i</u>**etly looked thro<u>u</u>gh the brush, the **hunt**ers left with the elk they had shot.

Grizzly 399 **be**gan **swim**ming **a**cross the river, **hop**ing to find some **tast**y elk **re**mains. As sh**e** swam **a**gainst the strong **cur**rent, her **bel**ly scr**a**ped **a**long the **riv**er **bot**tom. Sh**e** **e**merged from the **riv**er, **sha**king the **wa**ter from her thick c**o**at. **Quick**ly, sh**e** **dis**cov**ered** what was left of the elk. Sh**e** looked **a**round to **en**sure there were n**o** **hunt**ers **a**bout, and then sh**e** **start**ed to **e**at. Sh**e** **a**te a lot s**o** sh**e** could store **plen**ty of fat **be**fore **win**ter.

After **e**at**ing**, **Griz**zly 399 heard a noise and **spot**ted her **daugh**ter, 610, **ap**pr**o**ach**ing** with two of her cubs n**e**ar the spot of the **re**m**ai**n**ing car**cass.

Grizzly 399 **grunt**ed **loud**ly, **catch**ing her **daugh**ter's **at**ten**tion**. **Griz**zly 399 looked at 610's cubs; th**e**se were her **grand**chil**dren**.

Getting **Read**y for H**i**bern**a**tion

It was l**a**te Fall. Last Spring, **Griz**zly 399 had pushed her two cubs out of the den s**o** they could g**o** out on their **o**wn. Sh**e** taught them how to hunt and **pro**tect **them**selves from **pred**ators, **incl**u**d**ing large m**a**le be**a**rs, as well as **hu**mans. When they left, they were **pre**p**a**red to b**e** on their **o**wn.

Fall turned **in**to **Win**ter, and it was t**i**me for 399 to **re**turn to her den. Sh**e** **bur**r**o**wed thro**u**gh the sn**o**w **to**wards **Pil**grim Cr**ee**k, which fl**o**wed **be**low the **moun**tain where sh**e** denned. Once sh**e** r**e**ached her den, sh**e** dug it out, and soon **set**tled in the **moun**tain and fell **in**to a d**ee**p sl**ee**p.

Over the next **sev**eral days and nights, **Griz**zly 399 tossed and turned in her **moun**tain home. She **could**n't seem to get **com**fortable and was **unusually restless**. The next **morn**ing, she woke up with four cubs **nes**tled **be**side her. She was so **hap**py to have her new **ba**bies. **Griz**zly 399 loved **be**ing a mom!

As the **freez**ing **win**ter days wore on, **Griz**zly 399 **lis**tened to her cubs cry **loud**er and **loud**er. They were **get**ting **big**ger, and the den was **be**coming quite **crowd**ed! One day, she **de**cid**ed** to **ven**ture out to see if it was time to bring her cubs out of the den. When she went **out**side, she could smell the warm spring air and see the **melt**ing snow.

She **wait**ed a few more days **be**fore she **fi**nally brought her cubs out **in**to her great big world!

The New Cubs Meet Their World

"**Chil**dren," sh<u>e</u> said, "it's t<u>i</u>me to g<u>o</u> **out**s<u>i</u>de! <u>I</u> have **man**y **won**der**ful** things to sh<u>o</u>w yo<u>u</u>!" Sh<u>e</u> **e**merged from the den with the four cubs **tum**bling **be**h<u>i</u>nd her – one, two, thr<u>ee</u>, four. The **lit**tlest one **al**w<u>ay</u>s s<u>ee</u>med to b<u>e</u> last.

One of the cubs, **lat**er kn<u>o</u>wn as **Cu**ri<u>o</u>us, **be**cause h<u>e</u> was **VER**Y **in**quisitive, blinked his eyes and said, "**Mom**ma, the light is s<u>o</u> bright! <u>I</u> can **bare**ly s<u>ee</u>!"

D<u>o</u>n't **wor**ry! Your eyes will **ad**just to the **sun**light soon," sh<u>e</u> **re**plied.

The **oth**er cubs **sha**ded their eyes with their **lit**tle paws **un**til they could **fi**nal**ly** s<u>ee</u> their **sur**round**ings**.

"This **bea<u>u</u>tiful wil**der**ness** is your h<u>o</u>me for now," **Griz**zly 399 said. "**Fol**l<u>o</u>w m<u>e</u>, and <u>I</u>'ll sh<u>o</u>w it to y<u>ou</u>."

First, the gre**a**t **mom**ma **griz**zly took her cubs to the **riv**er for a c**o**ld, fresh drink of **wa**ter. Sh**e** **start**ed down the hill **to**wards the **riv**er with the cubs **fol**l**o**wing her as fast as their **lit**tle legs could **ca**rry them.

After they had **e**ach had **e**nough to drink, sh**e** said, "Now, **chil**dren, yo**u** must **fol**l**o**w m**e** **a**cross the **riv**er."

The four cubs looked at **e**ach **oth**er with f**e**ar in their eyes. The **fe**m**a**le cub, which **Griz**zly 399 called **Lit**tle **Mom**ma **be**cause sh**e** **al**w**a**ys **imit**a**t**ed her **moth**er, dipped her paw **in**to the c**o**ld **riv**er **wa**ter and **shiv**ered.

"**Mom**ma," sh**e** wh**i**ned, "it's so**ooo** c**o**ld! **I** can't swim **a**cross this w**i**de **riv**er!"

"Yes, yo**u** can," said **Mom**ma Be**a**r **stern**ly. "Yo**u** must **be**cause there's a lot of food on the **oth**er s**i**de. S**o**, let's g**o**!"

"Food? <u>O</u>h, yes, <u>I</u> will swim for food," **ex**cl<u>a</u>imed her **big**gest cub, **Hun**gry. **Griz**zly 399 n<u>a</u>med him **Hun**gry **be**cause h<u>e</u> **al**w<u>a</u>ys **wan**ted to <u>e</u>at.

"D<u>o</u>n't b<u>e</u> a **ba**by – yo<u>u</u> can do it - just watch m<u>e</u>," **Hun**gry t<u>o</u>ld **Lit**tle **Mom**ma. H<u>e</u> **be**gan to **fol**l<u>o</u>w **Griz**zly 399 **in**to the **wa**ter, but the **cur**rent of the **riv**er **start**ed to **c<u>a</u>r**ry him **down**str<u>e</u>am.

Momma said, "**Hun**gry, b<u>e</u> **care**ful! Watch m<u>e</u> – this is how yo<u>u</u> be<u>a</u>r **pad**dle," as sh<u>e</u> sh<u>o</u>wed him how to swim.

Hungry **imit<u>a</u>t**ed his **moth**er and **be**gan **swim**ming, **shout**ing to the **oth**ers, "Hey, look at m<u>e</u>. <u>I</u>'m **swim**ming!"

The **oth**er cubs **brav<u>e</u>**ly stepped **in**to the c<u>o</u>ld **riv**er to swim, **foll<u>o</u>wing Hun**gry's **exam**ple – all **ex**cept **Lit**tle **Mom**ma, who was **bawl**ing as sh<u>e</u> ran up and down the **riv**er**bank**.

The **lit**tle wet cubs and their **moth**er climbed out of the **riv**er **on**to the bank. **Hear**ing her **bawl**ing cub on the **oth**er side of the **riv**er, **Griz**zly 399 yelled, "I'm **com**ing **Lit**tle **Mom**ma!"

Looking at her drenched cubs, their **moth**er said, "Wait here while I get your **lit**tle **sis**ter."

Grizzly 399 swam back **a**cross the **riv**er and **gen**tly nudged **Lit**tle **Mom**ma **in**to the **wa**ter with her big snout. She swam **up**stream **along**side her **daugh**ter, so that her **mas**sive **bod**y blocked the strong **cur**rent, **ma**king it **eas**ier for **Lit**tle **Mom**ma to swim to her **broth**ers. Soon, the **en**tire bear **family** was **bask**ing in the warm sun on the **riv**er**bank**.

After their thick coats had dried a bit, **Griz**zly 399 said, "Time to go to the **mead**ow! We need to find food."

The Cubs Meet People
for the First Time

"Yay!" chimed the cubs. "We're **starving!**"

"Come **follow me**," **Griz**zly 399 told her cubs as they trailed close **be**hind her.

As the **grizzly family ap**proached the edge of the large **mead**ow, they **be**gan to hear **nois**es. Through the trees, they **spot**ted a crowd of **people stand**ing by the road, all **look**ing **to**ward them.

Curious **be**gan to shake her **lit**tle head. "**Mom**ma, what are those **animals** with two legs?"

Grizzly 399 **re**plied **calm**ly, "**Chil**dren, don't be scared. It's man. Don't fear him. Stay close to me and keep your **dis**tance. **Fol**low me as I teach you how to stay safe around **pe**ople."

Grizzly 399 walked **to**ward the **hu**mans to find a place to cross. As the bear **family** got **clos**er, a **si**lence fell over the crowd.

"That **mom**ma be<u>a</u>r is big and **beau**tiful," one **per**son **whis**pered in awe.

Another **per**son said **qui**etly, "<u>O</u>hhhh, look at the **lit**tle **ba**bi<u>es</u>!"

The **ex**c<u>it</u>ed crowd <u>a</u>imed their large **cam**eras and cell ph<u>o</u>nes at the **griz**zly be<u>a</u>r **fam**ily, **cap**turing this **won**der**ful** m<u>o</u>ment. CLICK, CLICK, CLICK, went the **cam**eras.

A Park **Ran**ger stood at the s<u>i</u>de of the r<u>o</u>ad, **wav**ing his arms and **sig**naling the **peo**ple to move back and **al**low the be<u>a</u>rs a s<u>a</u>fe **pas**sage**way**. H<u>e</u> pl<u>a</u>ced c<u>o</u>nes on **ei**ther s<u>i</u>de of the **ar**<u>ea</u> where the be<u>a</u>rs were **a**bout to cross and **in**struct**ed** **eve**ry**one** to st<u>a</u>y **out**s<u>i</u>de the c<u>o</u>nes' **bound**ari<u>es</u>.

H<u>e</u> **con**tin<u>u</u>ed to shout, "100 yards! Yo<u>u</u> must st<u>a</u>y 100 yards **a**w<u>a</u>y from the be<u>a</u>rs!"

Watching all the **com**m<u>o</u>**tion** on the r<u>o</u>ad, **Griz**zly 399 said, "**Re**mem**ber** my cubs, yo<u>u</u> must st<u>a</u>y **a**w<u>ay</u> from the **pe<u>o</u>**ple. W<u>e</u> d<u>o</u>n't kn<u>ow</u> if they're **friend**ly or not." Then sh<u>e</u> caught a **fa**mil**iar** scent and saw one man **stand**ing to the s<u>i</u>de, **h<u>o</u>ld**ing a **ver**y large **cam**era.

Sh<u>e</u> **rec**og**n<u>i</u>zed** him and knew h<u>e</u> was **friend**ly.

As the crowd **part**ed, the **r<u>a</u>ng**er felt a s<u>i</u>gh of **r<u>e</u>**lief as the **moth**er **griz**zly and her cubs **safe**ly crossed the r<u>o</u>ad.

Although the **b<u>a</u>**by cubs were **fr<u>i</u>ght**ened, they did **ex**act**ly** what their **moth**er had taught them. They had learned to **nav**i**g<u>a</u>te** and cross the r<u>o</u>ad **s<u>a</u>fe**ly, **d<u>e</u>**sp<u>i</u>te all the **ex**c<u>i</u>**ted on**look**ers**.

Grizzly 399 **Teach**es Her Cubs to F**i**nd Food

The **ba**by be**a**rs **foll**owed her **in**to the woods and **set**tled down to nurse.

Feeding four cubs was not **eas**y, as their **six**t**ee**n claws **some**t**i**mes dug **in**to her as they nursed.

When they **fin**ished **nurs**ing, sh**e** got up to look for bugs.

"Come, kids. There are lots of **tast**y bugs h**e**re to **e**at." **Griz**zly 399 **be**gan to **e**at them and the **sur**round**ing bal**sam roots.

Hungry chewed and m**a**de a **fun**ny f**a**ce, "Yuckkk! Th**e**se bugs t**a**ste **aw**ful. **I** want **some**thing else!" h**e** said.

Little **Mom**ma said, "Yo**u**'re s**o** **pick**y. **I** love to **e**at **what**ever **Mom**ma tells us to!"

During their first **sum**mer, **Griz**zly 399 taught them to eat the foods they found in the **for**est, in**clud**ing ber**ri**es, and roots, and how to hunt for small **an**imals and voles. She en**cour**aged them to find food in**dep**end**ently** even while they were still **nurs**ing. She al**so in**struct**ed** them to stay away from large male bears. She **point**ed out one bear and said, "That's your **fa**ther, but don't ap**proach** him. He's not **al**ways **ver**y nice."

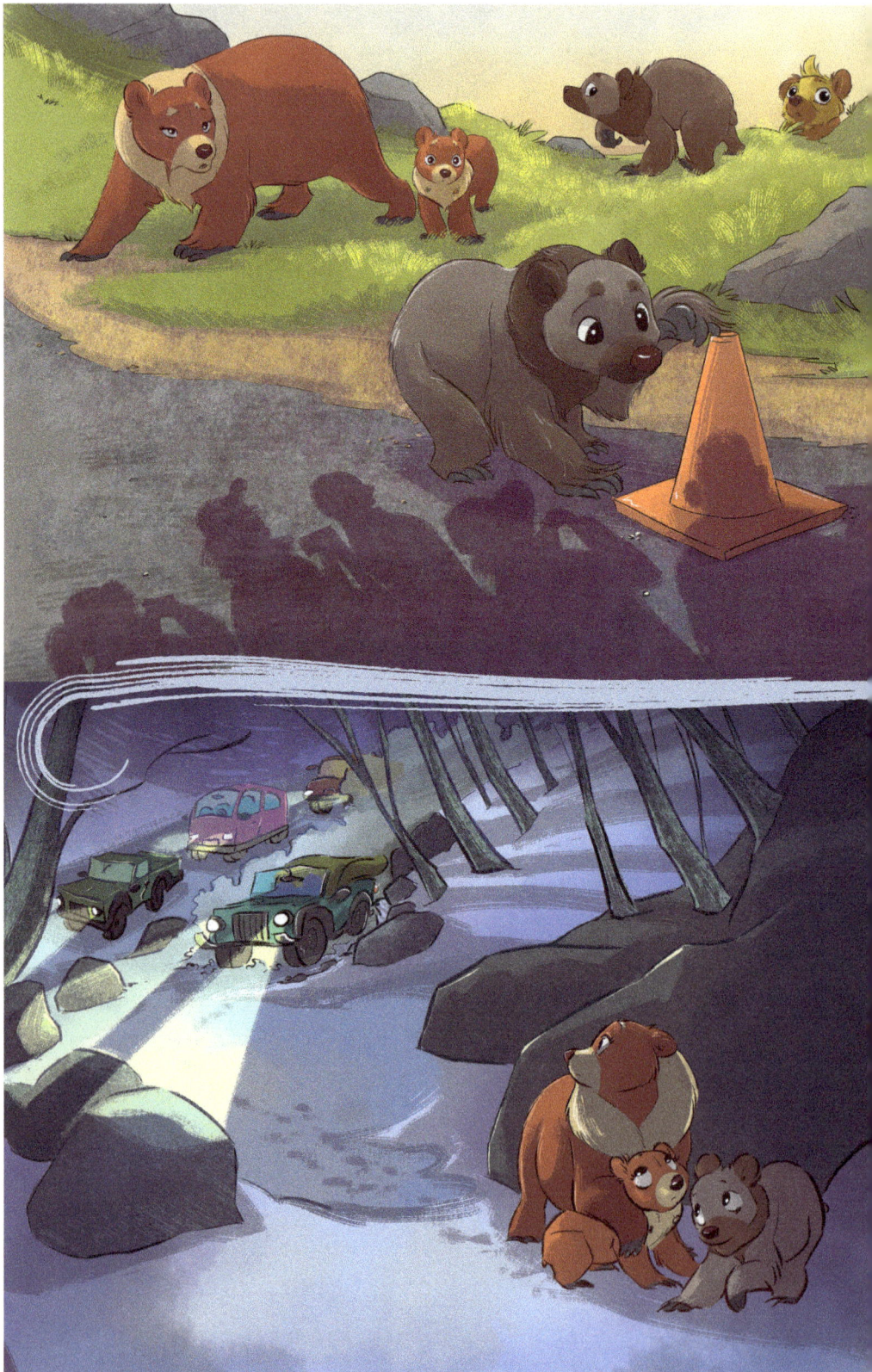

As the **sum**mer wore on, they saw crowds of **peo**ple lined up **a**long**side** the road. At times, it **was**n't **eas**y to get **a**round them, but the park **rang**ers were **usua**lly **pres**ent to help her **family** out.

She warned her cubs, "Don't get close to them!" **De**spite her **warn**ings, the cubs would **oc**ca**siona**lly get **cu**ri**ous** and **w a n** der **o**ver to smell the bright **or**ange cones placed on the side of the road. When this **hap**pened, **Mom**ma would get **up**set and call them over. **Ano**th**er** time, the bears were **leav**ing an **ar**ea where they had been **grub**bing for bugs when some **peo**ple in cars and trucks **be**gan **foll**o**wing** them **clo**se**ly. Mom**ma took the **ba**bies **a**way from there as **quick**ly as she could.

One d<u>ay</u> in **ear**ly fall, the cubs and their **mom**ma dug for **pock**et **go**phers in the **mead**<u>o</u>w.

Grizzly 399 looked <u>o</u>ver and saw **Hun**gry **dig**ging and **dig**ging **tire**lessly, in search of moths and roots, while **Sleep**y l<u>ay</u> **bask**ing in the sun.

Sh<u>e</u> paused her **grub**bing to count her cubs: "One, two, thr<u>ee</u> cubs. Where is **num**ber four? **Some**one's **miss**ing!"

Sh<u>e</u> called out to **Lit**tle **Mom**ma, "Where is **Cu**rious? As <u>u</u>s<u>ua</u>l, h<u>e</u>'s out of s<u>i</u>ght!" Then, they heard a noise. **Cu**rious was **try**ing to get **in**to a **squir**rel cache to steal some wh<u>i</u>te p<u>i</u>ne s<u>ee</u>ds.

Momma shook her head in **dis**b<u>e</u>li<u>e</u>f; sh<u>e</u> **could**n't **be**li<u>e</u>ve sh<u>e</u> had r<u>a</u>ised all of th<u>e</u>se **ba**by be<u>a</u>rs.

Sh<u>e</u> said to her cubs, "Kids, w<u>e</u> must start **eat**ing more to **pre**p<u>a</u>re for our long **win**ter sl<u>ee</u>p. W<u>e</u> won't have **an**y food wh<u>i</u>le we're **hi**bern**at**ing."

Hungry r<u>e</u>pli<u>e</u>d, "**O**k<u>ay</u>, **Mom**ma, **what**ever yo<u>u</u> s<u>ay</u>. **Af**ter all, <u>I</u> love to <u>e</u>at!"

Curious asked, "**Mom**ma, do w<u>e</u> have to sl<u>ee</u>p?"

"Yes, w<u>e</u> do," **Griz**zly 399 r<u>e</u>pli<u>e</u>d. "But **be**fore w<u>e</u> g<u>o</u>, let's g<u>o</u> find some **spe**cial tr<u>e</u>ats! **Re**mem**ber**, yo<u>u</u> must st<u>ay</u> cl<u>o</u>se to m<u>e</u> **be**cause **pe**<u>o</u>ple m<u>i</u>ght b<u>e</u> **near**by!"

Soon, they were **walk**ing down an **un**famil**i**ar dirt r**o**ad that led to an **ar**e**a** with lots of **hous**es where **pe**o**p**le lived.

They walked past **gar**bage cans with **o**pen lids and saw **o**ld food **ly**ing on top.

Hungry moved **to**ward the **gar**bage when **Mom**ma said, "N**o**, **Hun**gry, yo**u** must not get **in**to that **gar**bage can. That's **some**thing w**e** should **nev**er do."

As they **con**tin**ued walk**ing, **Mom**ma Bear sniffed the air and caught a whiff **com**ing from a tree. She **ap**proached the tree and **no**ticed **some**thing **hang**ing from its **branch**es.

It was a **wood**en box full of seeds.

"**Ba**bies, come here and taste the seeds," she said.

The **ba**bies **hur**ried over and **be**gan **eat**ing. When they **fin**ished, **Mom**ma bear **mo**tioned them to **fol**low her.

Once **a**gain, they **dis**cov**ered** more food. This time, the cubs **stumb**led **up**on a group of bee hives. They stuck their tongues and **nos**es in the hives and **tast**ed the sweet, **yum**my **hon**ey. Wow, what a great **ad**ven**ture**, thought **Mom**ma.

"I'm full now," **Sleep**y said. "I think I'm **read**y to take a nap!"

With **hon**ey smeared all over his face, **Hun**gry burped. "Good idea, but I must slurp up the rest of this **hon**ey!"

When they were **fin**ished, **Griz**zly 399 led her cubs back **in**to the woods, where they all napped in a **sun**ny **clear**ing.

After their nap, she took them even **fur**ther from their **for**est home to a place where men **hunt**ed elk and left the remains of the **car**cass**es**. The bears ate until **noth**ing remained.

Momma **an**nounced, "It's time to go back home."

Hungry said, "**Mom**ma, this was a **yum**my ad**ven**ture. **May**be we can do this again." **Mom**ma **nod**ded in ag**ree**ment.

39

The be**a**rs spent the rest of the fall **wan**der**ing be**tw**ee**n Grand **Te**ton **Nationa**l Park and the **near**by towns. They dug for roots and bugs, **find**ing **what**ever food they could **e**at to **pre**p**a**re for their long **hi**bern**a**tion. They **al**s**o** could not **re**sist r**o**am**ing the **ar**e**as** where **peo**ple lived, **search**ing for food that had been left out.

Some of their **fa**vor**ite** tr**e**ats were crab **ap**ples on the ground and horse f**ee**d. **E**ven **yum**mi**er** was the moose f**ee**d that **con**t**a**ined **molas**ses.

One time, **Hun**gry was **bus**y **try**ing to break **in**to a **bee**hive when he felt a jolt of **e**lectri**city** go through his coat.

He yelped and ran **a**way, **caus**ing his sisters, **broth**er, and **Griz**zly 399 to **be**come **fright**ened and run off as well.

In time, the wind blew cold, and once again, the sounds of **hunt**ers' guns **be**gan to **ech**o through the **val**leys.

The bears **lis**tened for these sounds and **wait**ed **un**til the **hunt**ers left. They would then find the **re**mains from the elk hunt and eat what was left.

If the **hunt**ers did not leave, **Griz**zly 399 would **sig**nal her cubs to **fol**low and hide from a **dis**tance **un**til they **de**part**ed**.

And **qui**etly they would wait.

43

Grizzly 399
Takes Her Cubs **in**to Town

One late **eve**ning, **Mom**ma Bear **an**nounced, "Kids, I have a gre**at** **i**de**a**. Let's g**o** check out the pl**a**ce full of **peo**ple. It's dark, and they **prob**ably w**o**n't s**ee** us. **Be**s**i**des, w**e** m**ay** find some **tast**y food!"

The young be**a**rs all l**i**ned up **be**hind their **moth**er to walk to the town of **Jack**son. When they **ar**r**i**ved, it was l**a**te at n**i**ght, and n**o** one s**ee**med to b**e** **a**round.

The **lit**tle be**a**rs sniffed the **a**ir and caught whiffs of all sorts of food, but they **ig**nored the smells **be**cause they had to k**ee**p up with their **Mom**ma **un**til sh**e** stopped **walk**ing.

She peered **in**to the **win**dow of a **build**ing with white cars parked **a**round it. **Sud**den**ly**, they heard **ve**hi**cles** with **flash**ing lights pull up **be**hind them.

Momma looked at the cars and said to her cubs, "It seems like they're **go**ing to **fol**low us. Let's leave. **Af**ter all, we don't **be**long here."

She held her head up high and walked **proud**ly out of town with her cubs **fol**low**ing clo**se**ly **be**hind her. The cars **fol**lowed them **un**til they reached the park.

Anyways, **Mom**ma thought. It's **a**bout time for us to go home!

Time to **Hibernate**

The snow was **fly**ing, and the wind was strong, but it was time for bed, and the bears had to make it back to their den.

Grizzly 399 broke ground through the deep snow so her cubs could **fol**low her more **eas**ily. They walked for miles, **strug**gling through the deep snow **un**til they **fi**nal**ly** reached the base of the **moun**tain.

"**Mom**ma, I'm tired! Can we take a quick rest?" **Lit**tle **Mom**ma asked, as the **oth**er cubs **nod**ded.

Grizzly 399 **re**plied, "**O**kay, just for a **lit**tle while. We're **al**most there – but we still have more work to do when we **ar**rive. We need to **pre**pare our den for our big sleep!"

With their big, **fluff**y c<u>o</u>ats, the **family be**gan to cl<u>i</u>mb the tall **moun**tain to r<u>e</u>ach their den.

When they **ar**r<u>i</u>ved, **Griz**zly 399 saw that the den was not large <u>e</u>nough to fit the wh<u>o</u>le **family**. Sh<u>e</u> knew they had to dig it out **un**til it was big <u>e</u>nough for all of them.

"<u>O</u>k<u>ay</u>, kids. Watch what <u>I</u> do," sh<u>e</u> said as sh<u>e</u> **en**tered the **fa**mil**iar** den sh<u>e</u> had <u>u</u>sed the **pr<u>e</u>vious** y<u>e</u>ar. She **be**gan to dig, and dirt flew out of the c<u>a</u>ve.

"Come help m<u>e</u>, cubs! There are f<u>i</u>ve of us now, and w<u>e</u> w<u>o</u>n't all fit. S<u>o</u>, w<u>e</u> have work to do!" sh<u>e</u> **ex**claimed.

The **lit**tle be<u>a</u>rs **com**pl<u>a</u>ined and sat down, t<u>i</u>red from their long walk. They **did**n't want to help but they knew they had to.

Final**ly**, they **fin**ished **dig**ging, and the young bears **en**tered the den with **Griz**zly 399, where they would sleep **to**geth**er warm**ly **un**til **win**ter was over.

"I will miss all that **yum**my food we had," **Hun**gry said as his **stom**ach **grum**bled.

"Us, too!" **a**greed his **broth**er and **sis**ters.

"Don't **wor**ry, **chil**dren," **Griz**zly 399 said. "When we wake up, you'll get to eat **a**gain. I'll teach you **eve**ry**thing** you need to know **un**til it's time for you to **en**ter the world on your own and have your **fam**ilies."

53

As sh**e** sp**o**ke, the **lit**tle be**a**rs **ex**cha**_**nged **wor**ri**e**d **glanc**es.

The five be**a**rs snoozed **clos**ely in their warm den wh**i**le sn**o**w **dust**ed the tr**ee**s.

Winter was long, and **Griz**zly 399 **of**ten dr**e**amed of **her**self and her **ba_**bi**e**s **snug**gling in their den. One n**i**ght, sh**e** **ven**tured out and sat **be**ne**a**th the br**i**ght, **shin**ing moon, **en**joy**ing** the **still**ness of the n**i**ght. As sh**e** sat **qui**etly in her **bea_u**ti**ful** **for**est h**o**me, thoughts of her cubs filled her m**i**nd. Sh**e** **won**dered what the next y**ea**r would bring for her and her **child**ren.

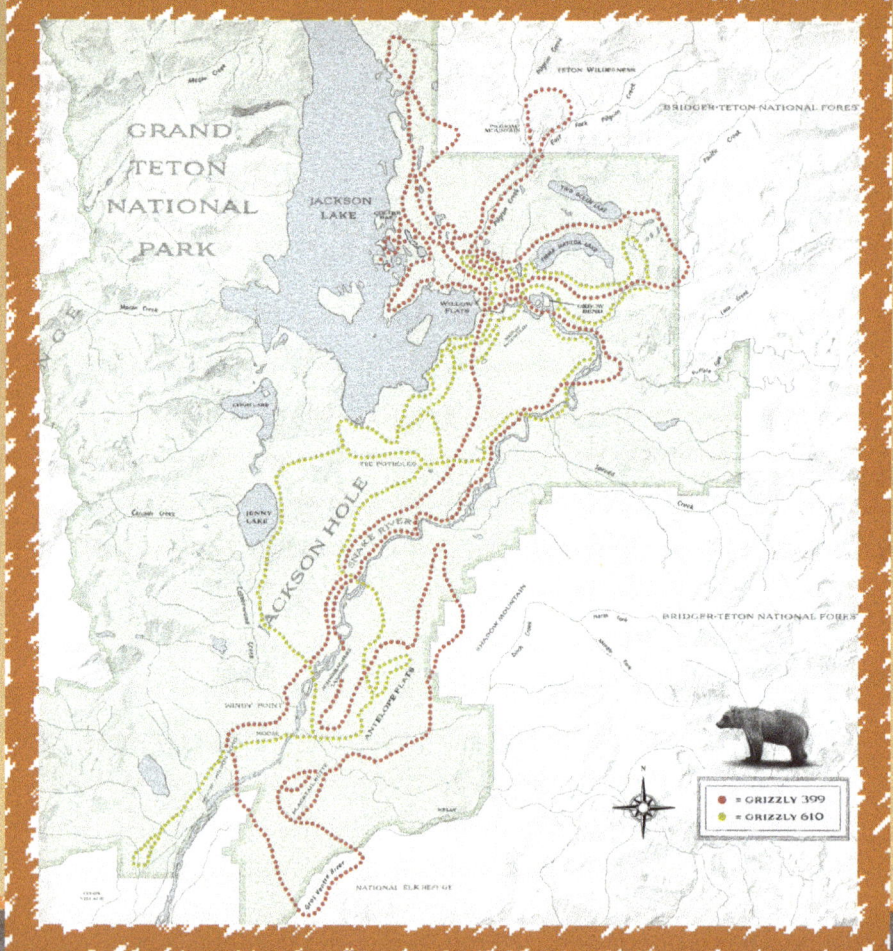

GRAND
TETON
NATIONAL
PARK

JACKSON LAKE

JACKSON HOLE

BRIDGER-TETON NATIONAL FOREST

BRIDGER-TETON NATIONAL FOREST

● = GRIZZLY 399
● = GRIZZLY 610

Science **Sec**tion

Grizzly 399

During the **Sum**mer and Fall of 2021, **Griz**zly 399 would take her cubs back and forth **be**tween Grand **Te**ton **Na**tional Park and **ar**eas as far as 60 miles south of their home in search of food left by **peo**ple. This **be**havior was quite **un**usual since she had not **ap**peared to take her cubs **in**to **ar**eas **pop**ulated by men in the past.

In the Spring of 2022, **Griz**zly 399 **sep**arated **her**self from her cubs, and the four cubs **ven**tured out on their own.

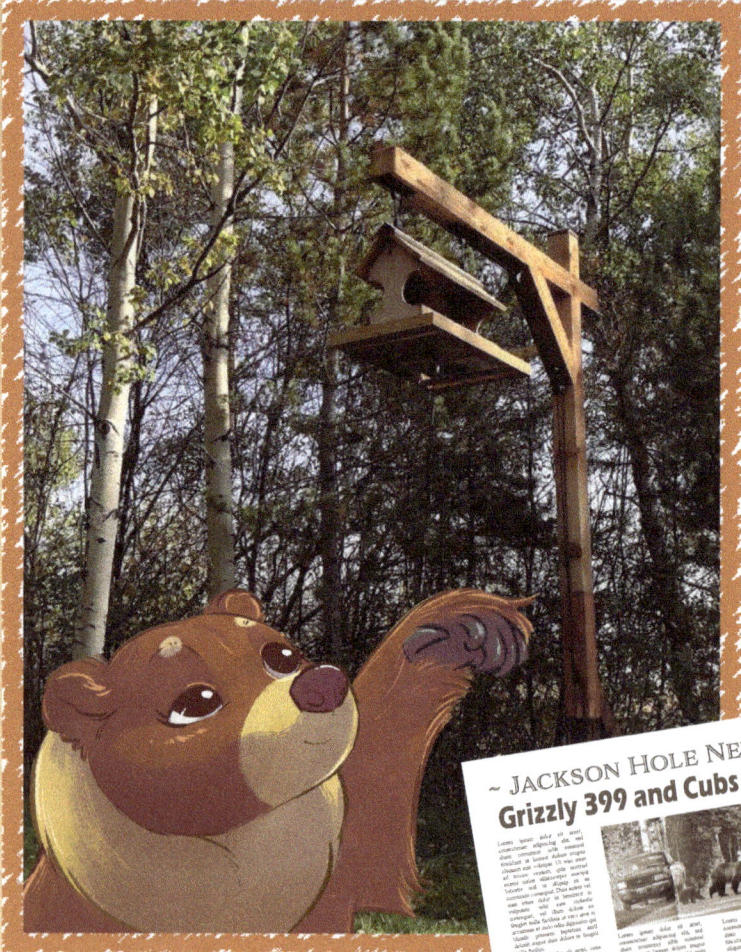

~ JACKSON HOLE NEWSPAPER~

Grizzly 399 and Cubs in Trouble!

Lorem ipsum dolor sit amet, consectetuer adipiscing elit, sed diam nonummy nibh euismod tincidunt ut laoreet dolore magna aliquam erat volutpat. Ut wisi enim ad minim veniam, quis nostrud exerci tation ullamcorper suscipit lobortis nisl ut aliquip ex ea commodo consequat. Duis autem vel eum iriure dolor in hendrerit in vulputate velit esse molestie consequat, vel illum dolore eu feugiat nulla facilisis at vero eros et accumsan et iusto odio dignissim qui blandit praesent luptatum zzril delenit augue duis dolore te feugait nulla facilisi.

Lorem ipsum dolor sit amet, consectetuer adipiscing elit, sed diam nonummy nibh euismod tincidunt ut laoreet dolore magna aliquam erat volutpat.

Lorem ipsum dolor sit amet, consectetuer adipiscing elit, sed diam nonummy nibh euismod tincidunt ut laoreet dolore magna aliquam erat volutpat. Ut wisi enim ad minim veniam, quis nostrud exerci tation ullamcorper.

Lorem ipsum dolor sit amet, consectetuer adipiscing elit, sed diam nonummy nibh euismod tincidunt ut laoreet dolore magna aliquam erat volutpat. Ut wisi enim ad minim veniam, quis nostrud exerci tation ullamcorper suscipit lobortis nisl.

Grizzly Bear Concerns

In 2021, **approximately** 29 **grizzly** bears were killed by the Fish & Game or **wildlife management**. This **oc**curred **be**cause the bears **be**came used to **hu**mans and **be**came food-**conditioned** due to **hu**mans' actions, **including** the availability of **live**stock. As a **re**sult, **many** of these bears **be**gan **visiting areas** where they could **easily ac**cess **hu**man food, which **ul**timately led to them **los**ing their lives.

What happens if we continue to **ha**bit**ua**te **grizzly** bears?

If we **con**tin**ue** down this path, bears will **possibly** be killed and their **families separat**ed. This is **already occurring**, and it could **also hap**pen to **Griz**zly 399, her cubs, and **oth**er **family mem**bers.

© THOMAS D. MANGELSEN

Additionally, livestock could be harmed, leading to more bears losing their lives.There is also the risk of people being injured.

Problem bears, as they are often referred to, may be relocated, which is confusing for them. This can put them in a dangerous situation because of potential conflicts with other grizzlies living in the same area.

When a bear gets too close to people, the rangers may need to use hazing techniques to scare them away. The bears don't like this and may not react well.

Adult bears and cubs that have become habituated may be taken from the wild and put in a sanctuary or zoo if they are not euthanized.

To k<u>ee</u>p **griz**zly be<u>a</u>rs s<u>a</u>fe,
h<u>o</u>meown**ers** and **vis**it**ors**
should **fol**l<u>o</u>w th<u>e</u>se **gu<u>i</u>de**lines:

- Do not l<u>ea</u>ve food out for dogs, cats, or **oth**er **animals**. F<u>ee</u>d pets **in**s<u>i</u>de and store pet food **in**s<u>i</u>de as well.
- **Re**move bird and **hum**ming**bird f<u>ee</u>d**ers or hang them at l<u>ea</u>st ten f<u>ee</u>t off the ground and four f<u>ee</u>t **a**w<u>a</u>y from the tr<u>ee</u> or p<u>o</u>le.
- Choose **hang**ing plants that **at**tract **hum**ming**birds**, but do not **at**tract be<u>a</u>rs.
- <u>U</u>se a be<u>a</u>r-**re**sist**ant** trash can or k<u>ee</u>p trash cans stored **in**s<u>i</u>de a **stur**dy **struc**ture **un**til the d<u>a</u>y of **pick**up.
- **A**void <u>o</u>ver**filli**ng trash cans. If the trash **does**n't fit, s<u>a</u>ve it **un**til the **fol**l<u>o</u>w**ing** w<u>ee</u>k or t<u>a</u>ke it to the dump.
- Store BBQ grills **in**s<u>i</u>de or cl<u>ea</u>n them well **af**ter <u>u</u>se.

For Ranch **Own**ers, **Bee**keep**ers**, and **Residents**

- <u>U</u>se **e**lec**tric fenc**ing **a**round **bee**h<u>i</u>ves, **chick**en coops, **gar**dens, and **com**p<u>o</u>st p<u>i</u>les.
- Store **l<u>i</u>ve**stock f<u>ee</u>d **in**doors.
- **Re**move fr<u>u</u>it from tr<u>ee</u>s, pick up **an**y **fall**en fr<u>u</u>it and **dis**p<u>o</u>se of it **proper**ly.
- **Re**move all salt and **min**eral blocks from your **proper**ty, or m<u>a</u>ke sure they are **in**acces**sible** to be<u>a</u>rs.

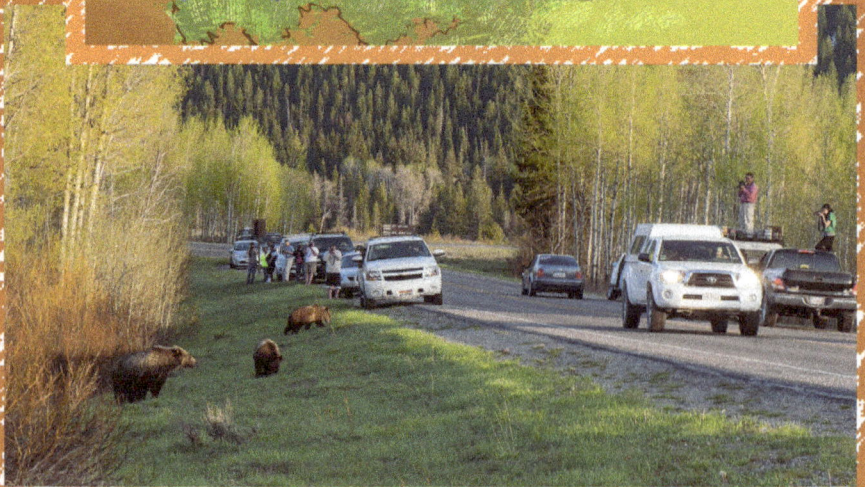

Personal **S**afety in **Griz**zly **Coun**try

What can you do to be safe or
avoid direct conflict with a bear?

- Don't leave food out and **un**attended. Securely store all food items.
- Avoid **tak**ing dogs while **hik**ing in bear **coun**try; if you do, keep your dogs on a leash.
- Hike in groups of three or more.
- Don't **sur**prise a bear! Make loud **nois**es; talk or sing while you hike to **a**lert bears to your **pres**ence.
- **Al**ways **car**ry bear spray. Keep it where you can **eas**ily **ac**cess it and not in your **back**pack.

Tips for **Ethical Wild**life **View**ing and **Pho**tography

- **Main**tain a safe **dist**ance – Stay at least 25 yards from all **wild**life, and 100 yards away from bears.
- **En**sure that you are **com**pletely pulled off the road, with all four tires **po**si**tioned** on the right-hand side of the white line.
- Do NOT **ap**proach or feed bears.
- Don't throw trash or food from a **ve**hicle. **Dis**pose of waste **pro**perly.
- Keep quiet – don't slam doors or speak **loud**ly, don't shout to get the **animals'** **at**ten**tion**. Do not intrude on their space.

- Drive **slow**ly and be **vigilant** for **wild**life, **allowing** time to stop if they **un**expect**edly** try to cross the road.
- **Al**ways stop and let bears cross the road **safe**ly.

Remember...
To be respectful of all wildlife,
as you're a guest in their home.

What is the **Sta**tus of **Griz**zly 399?

The **stor**y of **Griz**zly 399's has **cap**tiv**at**ed **man**y, **turn**ing her **in**to a **ce**lebr**i**ty bea**r**. This **pop**u**lar**ity has **in**spi**r**ed **doc**u**men**tary films, **nu**mer**ous ar**ticles, **a**dult and **chil**dren's books, and **e**ven her **o**wn **Face**book P**a**ge.

On M**a**y 16, 2023, **Griz**zly 399 **e**merged from **hi**bern**a**tion with a **beau**tiful cub, **lat**er kn**o**wn as **Spir**it. At the **a**ge of 26 or 27, sh**e be**c**a**me the **old**est kn**o**wn **griz**zly bea**r** to have cubs in the **Grea**ter **Yel**l**o**w**st**o**n**e **Ec**o**sys**tem (**GYE**).

    Tragica**lly**, on **Oct**o**ber** 22, 2024, while **Griz**zly 399 and her cub were **trav**eling **a**long a ro͟ad in the Snḁke **Riv**er **Can**yon, the **moth**er beḁr was struck and killed by a car. **Spir**it **sur**vi͟ved and **hope**fully found her wḁy back to **Te**͟ton **Nati**onal Park.

    There is ho͟pe that **Griz**zly 399's death will not be͟ in vḁin; the State of **Wy**o͟**ming** is **con**side**ring** **ex**pand**ing** the **num**ber of **wi**͟**ld**life **cross**ings such as o͟ver**pass**es, **un**der**pass**es, and **cul**verts to **re**d͟uce **wi**͟**ld**life-**ve**͟**hicle** hits.

This book is **dedicat**ed to **Griz**zly 399, her
cub **Spir**it, and all the **griz**zlies
she has helped to save by **be**ing an
ambassador to her **spe**cies.
We will miss her **great**ly.

- **Syl**via M. **Me**dina

Sound Key

How Noah Text® Works

Noah Text® allows readers to see sound-parts within words, providing a way for struggling readers to decode and enunciate words that are difficult to access. In turn, their improvement in reading accuracy and fluency frees up cognitive resources that they can devote to comprehending the meaning of the text, enabling them to truly enjoy reading while building their reading skills.

Syllables

A syllable is a unit of pronunciation with only one vowel sound, with or without surrounding consonants. Syllables line up with the way we speak and are an integrated unit of speech and hearing. Teachers often clap out syllables with their students.

Noah Text® acts upon words with more than one syllable. In a multiple-syllable word, the presentation of each syllable alternates bold, not bold, bold, etc. For example, the word "syllable" would be presented as "**syl**la**ble**," while the word "sound" is not changed at all.

Vowels

A long vowel is a vowel that pronounces its own letter name. Here are some examples of underlined long vowels you will find in Noah Text®, along with syllable breaks that are made obvious:

Long (a)

pl<u>a</u>te, p<u>ai</u>n, **hesit<u>a</u>te**, **n<u>a</u>**tion

h<u>ai</u>r, r<u>a</u>re, **par**ent, **l<u>i</u>**br<u>a</u>**ry**

p<u>a</u>le, f<u>ai</u>l, **de**t<u>a</u>il

tr<u>a</u>y, **al**w<u>a</u>ys

Long (e)

feet, teach, **com**plete

feel, deal, **ap**peal

ear, fear, here, **dis**ap**pear**, **se**vere

Long (i)

tribe, like, night, **high**light

fire, **ad**mire, **re**quire

mile, pile, **a**while, **rep**tile

Long (o)

globe, nose, **sup**pose, **re**mote

coach, whole, coal, goal, **ap**proach

mow, blown, **win**dow

Long (u)

huge, mule, **fu**el, **per**fume, **a**muse

hue, **ar**gue, **tis**sue, blue, **pol**lution

Disclaimer: As noted in the research provided at noahtext.com, the English writing system is extremely complex. Thus, the process of segmenting syllables, identifying rime patterns, and highlighting long vowels, is not only tedious but ambiguous at times based on the pronunciation of various regional dialects, the complexity of English orthography, and other articulatory considerations. Noah Text® strives to be as accurate as possible in developing clear, concise modified text that will assist readers; however, it cannot guarantee universal agreement on how all words are pronounced.

www.ingramcontent.com/pod-product-compliance
Lightning Source LLC
Chambersburg PA
CBHW052119030426
42335CB00025B/3057